AFTERNOON ON A HI[LL]

I will be the gladdest thing
    Under the sun!
I will touch a hundred flowers
    And not pick one.

I will look at cliffs and clouds
    With quiet eyes,
Watch the wind bow down the grass,
    And the grass rise.

And when lights begin to show
    Up from the town,
I will mark which must be mine,
    And then start down!

TO KATHLEEN

Still must the poet as of old,
In barren attic bleak and cold,
Starve, freeze, and fashion verses to
Such things as flowers and song and you;

Still as of old his being give
In Beauty's name, while she may live,
Beauty that may not die as long
As there are flowers and you and song.

For Lucy, whose feistiness is posilutely poetic & very Vincent.—J.M.F.

For the babies—Matthew, Mason, Otis, Luca, and Ivy.—E.V.

Starflower wouldn't exist without the scholarship and artistry of Dr. Nancy Milford's incomparable biography *Savage Beauty: The Life of Edna St. Vincent Millay*. We hold great admiration for Milford (1938–2022), who took thirty-one years to write this story, finding documents inside piano benches and researching from the road in her antique convertible.

We would also like to thank Patrick Kerwin at the Library of Congress for assisting us with essential research of archival images.

For my Arlo, whose zest for life, inquisitiveness, and curiosity continually gives me new eyes.

Thank you to the beautiful Maggie, Rosie, and Lola for bringing the Millay sisters to life.—J.D.

Text copyright © 2023 J. M. Farkas and Emily Vizzo
Illustrations copyright © 2023 Jasmin Dwyer

Photographs from the Millay Papers and poems ("Afternoon on a Hill," "To Kathleen," "Portrait by a Neighbor") by Edna St. Vincent Millay reprinted courtesy of Holly Peppe, Literary Executor, the Millay Society (millay.org).

Book design by Melissa Nelson Greenberg

Library of Congress Cataloging-in-Publication Data available.
ISBN: 978-1-951836-51-1

Printed in China

10 9 8 7 6 5 4 3 2 1

CAMERON KIDS is an imprint of CAMERON + COMPANY

CAMERON + COMPANY
Petaluma, California
www.cameronbooks.com

STARFLOWER

The Making of a Poet, Edna St. Vincent Millay

by J. M. Farkas & Emily Vizzo
illustrated by Jasmin Dwyer

cameron kids

Good things come in threes,
like peas like wishes like sisters.

Kathleen was the youngest & tenderest.
Norma, the middle, was singiest.
And Edna, the eldest, was fieriest
(her hair was red as her heart).

The Millays tangled in the bayberry bushes & queen of the
meadow, the hardhack & rose hips. Traded secret names
beneath the maple trees.

Indeed, those sisters were singular.
True like arrows, sparkle-dark as fireflies.

Some might say the Millay girls were haughty,
but they liked what they liked.
And what did they like best?
Too easy. They liked each other.

When Edna was born, her name was like a song:
Edna St. Vincent Millay—
but everyone called her Vincent.

Not all girls are named after a hospital in New York City,
Vincent told the rose hips.
I recognized the world right away.

Vincent learned to read from *Romeo and Juliet*; nothing less would do.

"Mother gave me poetry," she often said, as if poems were dandelions—
something bright & ferocious to hold in your hands.

Cora Lounella Buzzell was not like other mothers. She was
ambitious & unordinary & wanted the same for her daughters.

What other mother had better books than the library?
What other mother would steal the whole show?

Musical notes floated along the front porch.
"I'll take the chorus, you work the keys!" Mother called
from above dancing knees.

Edna St. Vincent Millay was only seven when she watched her father cross the cranberry bog to the railway station. Cora told Henry to go & never come back.

But Cora was brave. Who needed Henry anyway?

Camden, Maine: 100 Washington Street. The Millays moved to the smallest house on the loneliest road in the poorest part of town. Stenciled apple blossoms down the windowpanes, filled a pail of blueberries for supper.

Luckily the ocean was the biggest thing in the world. Wilder even than the woods! Every day swung open to a swoony new sea.

Not all girls eat salty air. But the Millay sisters did.

But what other mother was always away?

Cora had to earn a living. Buy meat for growing, hungry girls. As a nurse, she traveled for months at a time.

Alone at home, the girls felt almost like orphans. If they forgot to fill the lamps, they fumbled, lightless. If they didn't stoke the fire, they trembled in the cold.

Cold, cold. Forty-degrees-below cold. So cold your mouth could only hold one icy-blue word.

Until Vincent bloomed with an idea: *I'll tear off the roof.*
It wasn't much to scale those walls, kneel on the splintery
shingles & rip them away. What a cozy flame they made.

A miserable night is less miserable when your sisters share
the bed. Vincent's hair rivered warm across the pillows &
beneath the layered quilts.

They had a river once too. The Megunticook
was thrashy & rude. Sometimes the mills dyed
it daisy yellow & pennyroyal purple. In the
winter it would overflow, pushing past the front
door & freezing on the kitchen floor.

No mind. Those Millay sisters laced on skates
& made forever eights, whirled like tiny
tornadoes on that glassy rink. Trust Vincent to
carve her name with the edge of a silver blade.

True, the girls kept busy drawing birds & naming wildflowers,
but that's not the same as a mother.

Life is still better unbittered. Take it from Vincent!
She could divide the day like buttermilk cake.

Arise at six, breakfast at seven.
Busy hands among the plants not once
but *twice* a day.

Harvest boneset.
Pluck buttercups.
Glean lavender.
Arithmetic, iron, mend & mail.

Then:
Norma sorts buttons neatly in
silver tins.
Kathleen cleans the lima beans.
The Poet crushes flies.

Vincent had a private list:
Dream up sonnets.
Race her savage pen across the page,
rally unruly words & thorny lines.
(Sisters know to tiptoe when a poet's door is closed.)

OH WORLD,

I CANNOT

HOLD THEE

CLOSE ENOUGH!

Though the dishes never did wash themselves.
Stove untended, toast untoasted,
Vincent scribbled among her papers instead.

But you just never knew with Vincent.
She was moodier than the moon.
One moment she was sweet as peonies
& the next she thundered with rage.

One time her sister's mouth made Vincent so angry she
stuffed it with geranium leaves.

One time mad looked like a knife in a tree.

When sickness came the house turned sour. Nothing helped, not sherry, not oranges. Not even poems. A skyless, starless month. The sisters wilted, saw their shining hair fall out.

Mother finally returned until their fevers dimmed & her daughters got steadily better. Promised to dip her pencil in rubbing alcohol, send oven-baked letters.

And then, she was gone again.

Vincent lay her cheek against the organ's quiet keys.